chocolate
dreams

chocolate
dreams

Published by:
TRIDENT PRESS INTERNATIONAL
801 12th Avenue South, Suite 400
Naples, Fl 34102 USA
Tel: + 1 239 649 7077
Email: tridentpress@worldnet.att.net
Websites: www.trident-international.com
www.chefexpressinternational.com

Chocolate Dreams
© Trident Press International

Publisher
Simon St. John Bailey

Editor-in-chief
Isabel Toyos

Includes Index
ISBN 1582797625
UPC 6 15269 97625 8

2004 Edition
Printed in Colombia by Cargraphics S.A.

introduction

About chocolate, the Conquistadors of the New World say in their chronicles: **"After drinking it, you can travel entire days without fatigue or need for food."** They add: **"The beans are roasted and ground, then mixed with water to form a paste. This blend is heated till the cocoa butter rises to the surface, then mixed again and beat until a foamy liquid is formed to drink cooled."**

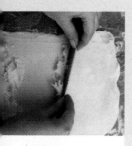

To this basic recipe the Aztecs would add chilies, vanilla sticks, pepper and cornflour. Later on, Oaxaca nuns improved the drink to suit Western taste, incorporating sugar, cinnamon and anis. And much later, the Indo American prime product reached sublime heights in the hands of European chocolate makers. By the middle of the nineteenth century the first chocolate industries had emerged, today's undisputable protagonists when it comes to preparing dream delights.

Tips and ideas

- **Melting:** Chocolate melts at body temperature; 36°C/96°F.
- **Molds:** To make molds check the temperature is right bringing lips close to the melted chocolate.
- **Chocolate leaves:** Easy to make coating with a brush melted chocolate on the backs of ivy leaves; once the chocolate has set, remove leaves, one at a time.

- **Small chocolate curls:** Scrape the chocolate tablet with a thin knife blade.
- **Big chocolate curls:** Spread melted chocolate on a flat surface; remove with spatula when hardened.
- **Bicolor decoration:** Sprinkle cacao on top of cake. Place a piece of cardboard over it, sprinkle glaze sugar and carefully remove cardboard.
- **Chocolate cream glaze:** To cover a cake, use 100 g/3 oz dark chocolate, 1 tablespoon water, 1 tablespoon glaze sugar and 100 ml/3 fl oz cream. Heat chocolate, cut in small pieces, and water, in low flame; when melted, add sugar and stir till mixture is smooth; finally, fold in cream, blending thoroughly.

Difficulty scale

■ □ □ I Easy to do

■ ■ □ I Requires attention

■ ■ ■ I Requires experience

the best
chocolate torte

■■■ | Cooking time: 45 minutes - Preparation time: 2 hours

ingredients

> 155 g/5 oz dark chocolate, broken into pieces
> 1 cup/170 g/5^1/2 oz brown sugar
> ^{1}/2 cup/125 ml/4 fl oz thickened cream (double)
> 2 egg yolks
> 200 g/6^1/2 oz butter, softened
> 1 cup/250 g/8 oz sugar
> 1 teaspoon vanilla essence
> 2 eggs, lightly beaten
> 1^1/2 teaspoons baking powder
> 2 cup/250 g/8 oz cake flour
> ^{3}/4 cup/185 ml/6 fl oz milk
> 3 egg whites

rich chocolate icing

> ^{3}/4 cup/185 g/6 oz sugar
> ^{3}/4 cup/185 ml/6 fl oz water
> 6 egg yolks
> 200 g/6^1/2 oz dark chocolate, melted
> 250g/8 oz butter, chopped

decorations

> 90 g/3 oz flaked almonds, toasted
> chocolate-drizzled strawberries

method

1. Place chocolate, brown sugar, cream and egg yolks in a heatproof bowl set over a saucepan of simmering water and cook, stirring constantly, until mixture is smooth. Remove bowl from pan and set aside to cool slightly.
2. Place butter, sugar and vanilla essence in a bowl and beat until light and fluffy. Gradually beat in eggs. Sift together flour and baking powder over butter mixture. Add chocolate mixture and milk and mix until well combined.
3. Place egg whites in a clean bowl and beat until stiff peaks form. Fold egg whites into chocolate mixture. Pour mixture into two greased and lined 23 cm/9 in round cake tins and bake at 180°C/350°F/Gas 4 for 40 minutes or until cakes are cooked when tested with a skewer. Stand cakes in tins for 5 minutes before turning onto wire racks to cool.
4. To make icing, place sugar and water in saucepan and heat over a low heat, stirring constantly, until sugar dissolves. Bring to the boil, then reduce heat and simmer for 4 minutes or until mixture is syrupy.
5. Place egg yolks in a bowl and beat until thick and pale. Gradually beat in sugar syrup and melted chocolate. Then gradually beat in butter and continue beating until mixture is thick. Cover and refrigerate until icing is of a spreadable consistency.
6. To assemble torte, split each cake horizontally. Place one layer of cake on a serving plate and spread with icing. Top with

a second layer of cake and icing. Repeat layers to use remaining cake. Spread top and sides of cake with remaining icing. Press almonds into sides of torte and decorate top with chocolate-drizzled strawberries.

....
Serves 10-12

tip from the chef

To prepare the strawberries, wash, pat dry and place berries on a tray. Pipe thin lines of melted dark or white chocolate back and forth across the strawberries and let stand until set.

the best
mud cake

■■□ | Cooking time: 45 minutes - Preparation time: 45 minutes

method

1.Place chocolate, caster sugar and butter in a heatproof bowl (a) set over a saucepan of simmering water and heat, stirring, until mixture is smooth. Remove bowl and set aside to cool slightly. Beat in egg yolks (b) one at a time, beating well after each addition. Fold in flour.

2.Place egg whites in a clean bowl and beat until stiff peaks form. Fold egg whites into chocolate mixture (c). Pour mixture into a greased 23 cm/9 in springform tin and bake at 180°C/350°F/Gas 4 for 45 minutes or until cake is cooked when tested with a skewer. Cool cake in tin.

3.Just prior to serving dust cake with cocoa powder and icing sugar.

Makes one 23 cm/9 in round cake

ingredients

> **350 g/11 oz dark chocolate, broken into pieces**
> **3/4 cup/170 g/5 1/2 oz caster sugar**
> **185 g/6 oz butter, chopped**
> **5 eggs, separated**
> **1/3 cup/45 g/1 1/2 oz flour, sifted**
> **cocoa powder, sifted**
> **icing sugar, sifted**

tip from the chef

To bake a light cake, always add the beaten egg whites at the end, folding them in gently with down-up-over motion.

a

b

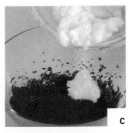

c

devil's
food cake

■ ■ ■ | Cooking time: 25 minutes - Preparation time: 60 minutes

ingredients

> 1 cup/100 g/3¹/2 oz cocoa powder
> 1¹/2 cups/375 ml/ 12 fl oz boiling water
> 375 g/12 oz unsalted butter, softened
> 1 teaspoon vanilla essence
> 1¹/2 cups/330 g/ 10¹/2 oz caster sugar
> 4 eggs
> 2¹/2 cups/315 g/10 oz flour
> ¹/2 cup/60 g/2 oz cornflour
> 1 teaspoon bicarbonate of soda
> 1 teaspoon salt
> ¹/2 cup/125 ml/4 fl oz cream (double), whipped

chocolate butter icing

> 250 g/8 oz butter, softened
> 1 egg
> 2 egg yolks
> 1 cup/155 g/5 oz icing sugar, sifted
> 185 g/6 oz dark chocolate, melted and cooled

method

1. Blend cocoa powder and water in a bowl. Set aside to cool. Place butter and vanilla essence in a bowl and beat until light and fluffy. Gradually add caster sugar, beating well after each addition until mixture is creamy. Beat in eggs one at a time, beating well after each addition.

2. Sift together flour, cornflour, bicarbonate of soda and salt. Fold flour mixture and cocoa mixture, alternately.

3. Divide batter between three greased and lined 23 cm/9 in sandwich tins and bake at 180°C/350°F/Gas 4 for 20-25 minutes or until cakes are cooked when tested with a skewer. Stand in tins for 5 minutes before turning onto wire racks to cool completely.

4. To make icing, place butter in a bowl and beat until light and fluffy. Mix in egg, egg yolks and icing sugar. Add chocolate and beat until icing is thick and creamy. Sandwich cakes together using whipped cream, then cover top and sides with icing.

Makes a 23 cm/9 in round cake

tip from the chef

Chocolate "seizes" if it is overheated or if it comes in contact with water or steam. Seizing results in the chocolate tightening. To rescue seized chocolate, stir a little cream or vegetable oil into the chocolate until it becomes smooth again.

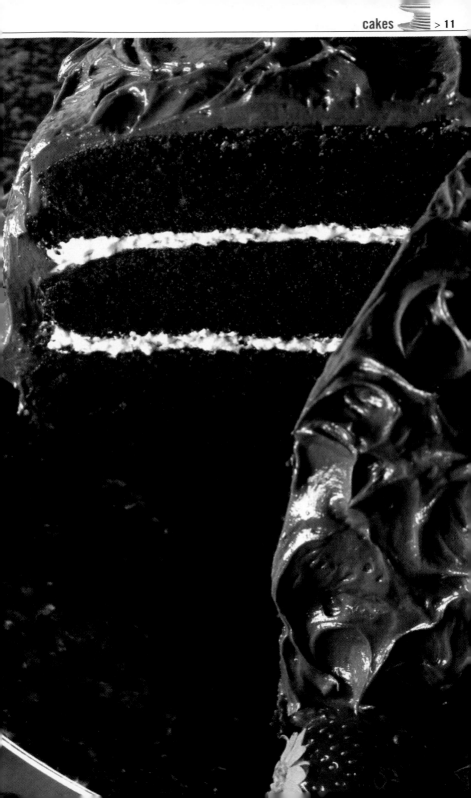

chocolate
pound cake

■ ☐☐ I Cooking time: 55 minutes - Preparation time: 20 minutes

method

1. Place butter, sugar and vanilla essence in a bowl and beat until light and fluffy. Gradually beat in eggs.
2. Sift together baking powder, flour and cocoa powder. Fold flour mixture and milk, alternately, into butter mixture.
3. Pour mixture into a greased and lined 20 cm/8 in square cake tin and bake at 190°C/375°F/Gas 5 for 55 minutes or until cake is cooked when tested with a skewer. Stand cake in tin for 10 minutes before turning onto a wire rack to cool.

ingredients

> 185 g/6 oz butter, softened
> 1^1/2 cups/330 g/ 10^1/2 oz caster sugar
> 3 teaspoons vanilla essence
> 3 eggs, lightly beaten
> 2 cups/250 g/8 oz plain flour
> 2 teaspoons baking powder
> ^{1}/2 cup/45 g/1^1/2 oz cocoa powder
> 1^1/4 cups/315 ml/ 10 fl oz milk

Makes one 20 cm/8 in square cake

tip from the chef

This rich buttery cake can be served plain, with a readymade chocolate sauce or with cream. A simple glacé icing drizzled over the top makes another delicious alternative.

chocolate
brownie torte

■□□ | Cooking time: 20 minutes - Preparation time: 25 minutes

ingredients

> 185 g/6 oz dark chocolate, roughly chopped
> 45 g/1½ oz butter, chopped
> ¼ cup/60 g/2 oz caster sugar
> 1 egg
> ½ teaspoon vanilla essence
> 60 g/2 oz slivered almonds
> ¼ cup/30 g/1 oz flour
> 6 scoops ice cream, flavor of your choice

method

1. Place 125 g/4 oz chocolate and butter in a heatproof bowl over a saucepan of simmering water and heat, stirring, for 5 minutes or until chocolate melts and mixture is smooth.

2. Place sugar, egg and vanilla essence in a bowl and beat until mixture is thick and creamy. Beat in chocolate mixture, then fold in almonds, flour and remaining chocolate pieces. Spoon mixture into a lightly greased and lined 20 cm/8 in sandwich tin and bake at 180°C/350°F/Gas 4 for 15-20 minutes or until cooked when tested with a skewer. Turn onto a wire rack and cool for 5-10 minutes before serving.

3. To serve, cut warm brownie into wedges and accompany with a scoop of ice cream —coffee-flavored ice cream is a delicious accompaniment for this dessert.

Serves 6

tip from the chef

Chocolate melts more rapidly if broken into small pieces. The melting process should occur slowly, as chocolate scorches if overheated. The container in which chocolate is being melted should be kept uncovered and completely dry. Covering could cause condensation and just one drop of water will ruin the chocolate.

chocolate
sandwich cake

■■□ | Cooking time: 25 minutes - Preparation time: 45 minutes

method

1. Place flour, bicarbonate of soda, cocoa powder, butter, sugar, eggs and sour cream in a large mixing bowl and beat until well combined and mixture is smooth.
2. Spoon batter into two greased and lined 20 cm/8 in sandwich tins and bake at 180°C/350°F/Gas 4 for 25-30 minutes or until cooked when tested with a skewer. Stand cakes in tins for 5 minutes before turning onto a wire rack to cool.
3. Sandwich cold cakes together with whipped cream.
4. To make icing, place chocolate and butter in a small saucepan and cook over a low heat, stirring constantly, until melted. Cool slightly then spread over top of cake.

Makes a 20 cm/8 in sandwich cake

ingredients

> 1 cup/125 g/4 oz self-raising flour, sifted
> 1/4 teaspoon bicarbonate of soda
> 1 cup/45 g/11 1/2 oz cocoa powder, sifted
> 3/4 cup/170 g/5 1/2 oz caster sugar
> 1/2 cup/125 ml/4 fl oz cream (double), whipped
> 125 g/4 oz butter, softened
> 2 eggs, lightly beaten
> 1 cup/250 g/8 oz sour cream

chocolate icing

> 60 g/2 oz dark chocolate, chopped
> 30 g/1 oz unsalted butter

tip from the chef

To frost only the top of the cake leaving the sides free, cool glaze to spreading consistency; this will make it easier to pour gradually over the top and spread with a spatula.

chocolate
hazelnut torte

■■□ I Cooking time: 50 minutes - Preparation time: 50 minutes

ingredients
> 250 g/8 oz dark chocolate, broken into pieces
> 6 eggs, separated
> 1 cup/250 g/8 oz sugar
> 315 g/10 oz hazelnuts, toasted and roughly chopped
> 1 tablespoon rum
> icing sugar, sifted

method
1. Place chocolate in a heatproof bowl set over a saucepan of simmering water and heat, stirring, until chocolate melts. Remove bowl from pan and let cool slightly.
2. Place egg yolks and sugar in a bowl and beat until thick and pale. Fold chocolate, hazelnuts and rum into egg mixture.
3. Place egg whites into a clean bowl and beat until stiff peaks form. Fold egg whites into chocolate mixture. Pour mixture into a greased and lined 23 cm/9 in springform tin and bake at 190°C/375°F/Gas 5 for 50 minutes or until cake is cooked when tested with a skewer. Cool cake in tin. Dust cake with icing sugar just prior to serving.

Serves 8

tip from the chef
For a tempting twist to this glaze, prepare a quick topping mixing 100 g/3¹/₂ oz white chocolate with 50 g/1³/₄ oz butter; spread gradually over the top using a spatula.

berry chocolate mud cake

■ ■ □ | Cooking time: 75 minutes - Preparation time: 45 minutes

method

1. Place chocolate and butter in a heatproof bowl over a saucepan of simmering water and heat, stirring, until chocolate melts and mixture is smooth. Cool slightly.
2. Beat egg yolks and caster sugar into chocolate mixture, then fold in flour.
3. Place egg whites in a separate bowl and beat until stiff peaks form. Fold egg whites and raspberries into chocolate mixture. Pour into a greased and lined 20 cm/8 in round cake tin and bake at 120°C/250°F/Gas ¹/₂ for 1¹/₄ hours or until cooked when tested with a skewer. Turn off oven and cool cake in oven with door ajar.
4. To make coulis, place raspberries in a food processor or blender and process until puréed. Push purée through a sieve to remove seeds. Add sugar to taste. Serve cake with coulis and cream.

ingredients

> 315 g/10 oz dark chocolate
> 250 g/8 oz butter, chopped
> 5 eggs, separated
> 2 tablespoons caster sugar
> ¹/₄ cup/30 g/1 oz self-raising flour, sifted
> 250 g/8 oz raspberries
> whipped cream, for serving

raspberry coulis

> 250 g/8 oz raspberries
> sugar to taste

Serves 10

tip from the chef

To simplify preparation of coulis, dilute ¹/₂ cup strawberry or raspberry jam in 2 tablespoons water. This express sauce saves time and is equally tasty.

chocolate
date torte

■■□ I Cooking time: 40 minutes - Preparation time: 45 minutes

ingredients
> **6 egg whites**
> **1 cup/220 g caster sugar**
> **200 g/6¹/₂ oz dark chocolate, grated**
> **160 g/5 oz pitted dates, chopped**
> **2 cups/280 g chopped hazelnuts**
> **1¹/₂ cups/375 ml thickened cream, whipped**

topping
> **100 g/3¹/₂ oz dark chocolate, melted**

method
1. Beat egg whites until soft peaks form. Gradually add sugar and beat until dissolved. Fold in chocolate, dates and hazelnuts.
2. Spoon mixture into two greased and lined 23 cm/9 in springform pans. Bake at 160°C/325°/Gas 3 for 40 minutes or until firm. Remove from oven and allow to cool in pans.
3. Spread one meringue layer with whipped cream and top with remaining layer. Decorate top with drizzled melted chocolate.

....
Serves 12

tip from the chef
To make the cake even more chocolatey, fill with a mixture of fluffy whipped cream and 2 tablespoons cocoa powder.

chocolate
shortcake

■□□ I Cooking time: 10 minutes - Preparation time: 15 minutes

method

1. Melt chocolate in a microwavable bowl on Defrost (microwave power 30%) for 2 minutes, stir, then heat for 2 minutes longer. Continue in this way for 6-8 minutes longer or until chocolate is completely melted.

2. Stir shortbread into chocolate, then add sour cream or cream, almonds or hazelnuts and liqueur, if using, and mix well to combine.

3. Press mixture in a base-lined and buttered 18 cm/7 in diameter round cake tin and chill until firm.

Makes an 18 cm/7 in round cake

ingredients

> **200 g/6¹/2 oz dark cooking chocolate, broken into small pieces**
> **100 g/3¹/2 oz shortbread finger biscuits, cut into chunky pieces**
> **¹/2 cup/125 g/4 oz sour cream or ¹/2 cup/125 ml/4 fl oz cream (double)**
> **¹/4 cup/60 g/2 oz ground almonds or hazelnuts**
> **1 tablespoon orange-flavored or whiskey liqueur (optional)**

tip from the chef

This is a quick and slick treat for chocoholics who don't want to spend a lot of time in the kitchen. Serve cut into wedges for morning coffee or afternoon tea or with sugared berries for a simple dessert.

chocolate
almond cake

■□□ | Cooking time: 30-40 minutes - Preparation time: 10 minutes

ingredients

> **30 g/1 oz finely chopped almonds**
> **1/4 cup/45 g/1 1/2 oz brown sugar**
> **1 packet rich chocolate cake mix**

strawberry sauce
> **250 g/8 oz strawberries**
> **1 tablespoon strawberry jam**
> **1 tablespoon lemon juice**

method

1. Place almonds and sugar in a small bowl and mix to combine. Sprinkle sugar mixture over the base of a greased and lined 11 x 21 cm/4 1/2 x 8 1/2 in loaf tin.
2. Make up packet cake following packet directions. Pour batter into loaf tin and bake according to packet directions.
3. To make sauce, place strawberries, jam and lemon juice in a food processor or blender and process until smooth. Push mixture through a sieve and discard any pips.
4. Allow cake to stand in tin for 5 minutes before turning out. To serve, cut into slices and accompany with sauce.

....
Serves 8

tip from the chef

An easy way to make a packet cake mix into something special. You can use any nuts that you like in place of the almonds. Why not try ground hazelnuts or shredded coconut for something different?

triple-chocolate
terrine

■■■ | Cooking time: 35 minutes - Preparation time: 2 hours

method

1. To make cake, place butter and vanilla essence in a bowl and beat until light and fluffy. Gradually beat in sugar and continue beating until mixture is creamy. Beat in eggs one at a time. Fold flour and milk, alternately, into butter mixture. Spoon mixture into a greased and lined 11 x 21 cm/4¹/2 x 8¹/2 in loaf tin and bake at 180°C/350°F/Gas 4 for 20-25 minutes or until cooked when tested with a skewer. Stand in tin for 5 minutes, then turn onto a wire rack to cool.

2. To make fudge filling, place butter and icing sugar in a bowl and beat until creamy. Fold in dark chocolate and cream. Chill until required.

3. To make mousse, place milk chocolate and butter in a saucepan and cook over a low heat, stirring constantly, until well blended. Cool. Place sugar and eggs in a bowl and beat until thick and creamy. Fold in chocolate mixture, cream, rum and gelatin mixture.

4. To assemble terrine, cut cake horizontally into three layers. Spread 2 layers with fudge filling and place one of these layers, filling side up, in the base of an 11 x 21 cm/ 4¹/2 x 8¹/2 in loaf tin lined with plastic food wrap. Top with half the mousse and chill for 10 minutes or until almost set. Place the second layer of filling-topped cake over the mousse with filling facing upwards. Top with remaining mousse and chill until

ingredients

butter cake
> 125 g/4 oz butter
> 1 teaspoon vanilla essence
> ¹/2 cup/100 g/3¹/2 oz caster sugar
> 2 eggs
> 1 cup/125 g/4 oz self-raising flour, sifted
> ¹/3 cup/90 ml/3 fl oz milk

chocolate fudge filling
> 125 g/4 oz butter
> 2 tablespoons icing sugar
> 90 g/3 oz dark chocolate, melted and cooled
> 1 cup/250 ml/8 fl oz cream (double), chilled

milk chocolate mousse
> 200 g/6¹/2 oz milk chocolate, chopped
> 125 g/4 oz unsalted butter
> 2 tablespoons caster sugar
> 2 eggs
> 1 cup/250 ml/8 fl oz cream (double)
> 1 tablespoon dark rum
> 6 teaspoons gelatin dissolved in 2 tablespoons hot water, cooled

white chocolate glaze
> 250 g/8 oz white chocolate
> 100 g/3¹/2 oz unsalted butter

triple-chocolate
terrine

almost set. Place remaining cake layer on top and chill until set.

5. To make glaze, place white chocolate and butter in a saucepan and cook over a low heat, stirring constantly, until well blended. Cool slightly. Turn terrine onto a wire rack, trim edges, pour over glaze (a) to cover. Allow to set.

....

Serves 10

tip from the chef

Chocolate should be stored in a dry, airy place at a temperature of about 16°C/32°F. If stored in unsuitable conditions, the cocoa butter in chocolate may rise to the surface, leaving a white film. A similar discoloration occurs when water condenses on the surface. This often happens to refrigerated chocolates that are too loosely wrapped. Chocolate affected in this way is still suitable for melting, however it is unsuitable for grating.

a

black-and-white
tart

black-and-white
tart

■ ■ ■ | Cooking time: 25 minutes - Preparation time: 90 minutes

ingredients

macaroon shell
> **2 egg whites**
> **$^1/_2$ cup/100 g/3$^1/_2$ oz caster sugar**
> **220 g/7 oz desiccated coconut**
> **$^1/_4$ cup/30 g/1 oz flour, sifted**

chocolate sour cream filling
> **2 egg yolks**
> **$^3/_4$ cup/185 ml/6 fl oz thickened double cream**
> **185 g/6 oz dark chocolate**
> **2 tablespoons cognac or brandy**
> **185 g/6 oz white chocolate**
> **$^2/_3$ cup/155 g/5 oz sour cream**

raspberry coulis
> **250 g/8 oz raspberries**
> **1 tablespoon icing sugar**

method

1. Place egg whites in a bowl and beat until soft peaks form. Gradually beat in caster sugar. Fold in coconut and flour (a). Press mixture over base and up sides of a greased and lined 23 cm/9 in round flan tin with a removable base (b). Bake at 180°C/350°F/Gas 4 for 20-25 minutes or until golden. Stand in tin for 5 minutes then remove and place on a wire rack to cool.

2. To make filling, place egg yolks and cream (c) in a heatproof bowl set over a saucepan of simmering water and beat until thick and pale. Stir in dark chocolate (d) and cognac or brandy and continue stirring until chocolate melts (e). Remove bowl from pan and set aside to cool.

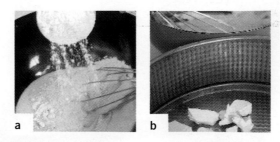

a   b

3. Place white chocolate and sour cream in a heatproof bowl set over a saucepan of simmering water and heat, stirring, until mixture is smooth. Remove bowl from pan and set aside to cool.

4. Place alternating spoonfuls of dark and white mixtures in macaroon shell and, using a skewer, swirl mixtures to give a marbled effect. Chill for 2 hours or until filling is firm.

5. To make coulis, place raspberries in a food processor or blender and process to make a purée. Press purée through a sieve to remove seeds, then stir in icing sugar. Serve with tart.

....
Serves 8

tip from the chef

This dessert is best served the day it is made as the macaroon shell may absorb too much moisture on standing and lose its crispness.

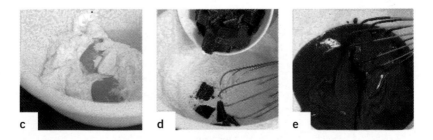

c   d   e

raspberry
truffle cakes

■■■ | Cooking time: 32 minutes - Preparation time: 70 minutes

ingredients

> 1/2 cup/45 g/1 1/2 oz cocoa powder, sifted
> 1 cup/250 ml/8 fl oz boiling water
> 1 3/4 cups/400 g/ 12 1/2 oz caster sugar
> 125 g/4 oz butter
> 1 1/2 tablespoons raspberry jam
> 2 eggs
> 1 2/3 cups/200 g/ 6 1/2 oz self-raising flour, sifted
> 410 g/13 oz dark chocolate, melted
> raspberries for garnishing

raspberry cream

> 125 g/4 oz raspberries, puréed and sieved
> 1/2 cup/125 ml/4 fl oz cream (double), whipped

chocolate sauce

> 125 g/4 oz dark chocolate
> 1/2 cup/125 ml/4 fl oz water
> 1/4 cup/60 g/2 oz caster sugar
> 1 teaspoon brandy (optional)

method

1. Dissolve cocoa powder in boiling water, then cool.
2. Place sugar, butter and jam in a bowl and beat until light and fluffy. Beat in eggs one at a time, adding a little flour with each egg. Fold remaining flour and cocoa mixture, alternately, into butter mixture.
3. Spoon mixture into eight lightly greased 1/2 cup/125 ml/4 fl oz capacity ramekins or large muffin tins. Bake at 180°C/350°F/Gas 4 for 20-25 minutes or until cakes are cooked when tested with a skewer. Stand cakes in tins for 5 minutes then turn onto wire racks to cool. Turn cakes upside down and scoop out centre (a) leaving a 1 cm/1/2 in shell. Spread each cake with chocolate to cover top and sides, then place right way up on a wire rack.
4. To make cream, fold raspberry purée into cream. Spoon cream into a piping bag fitted with a large nozzle. Carefully turn cakes upside down and pipe in cream (b) to fill cavity. Place right way up on individual serving plates.
5. To make sauce, place chocolate and water in a saucepan and cook over a low heat, stirring, for 4-5 minutes or until chocolate melts. Add sugar and continue cooking, stirring constantly, until sugar dissolves. Bring just to the boil, then reduce heat and simmer, stirring, for 2 minutes. Cool for 5 minutes, then stir in brandy, if using. Cool sauce to room temperature and serve with cakes.

....
Serves 8

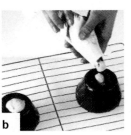

tip from the chef

These rich little chocolate cakes filled with a raspberry cream and served with a bittersweet chocolate sauce are a perfect finale to any dinner party.

the ultimate
chocolate sundae

■■□ | Cooking time: 40 minutes - Preparation time: 40 minutes

method

1. To make base, place butter, eggs, caster sugar and vanilla essence in a bowl and beat to combine. Add flour, cocoa powder, dates and pecans and mix well to combine.

2. Pour mixture into a greased and lined 20 cm/8 in-square cake tin and bake at 180°C/350°F/Gas 4 for 30 minutes or until firm to touch, but still fudgey in the center. Cool in tin, then cut into six squares.

3. To make sauce, place brown sugar, cocoa powder, cream and butter in a saucepan and cook over a low heat, stirring constantly, until sugar dissolves. Bring to the boil, then reduce heat and simmer for 5 minutes or until sauce thickens slightly.

4. To assemble sundaes, top each brownie square with a scoop of vanilla, chocolate and choc-chip ice cream. Drizzle with hot sauce and serve.

....
Serves 6

ingredients

> **6 scoops vanilla ice cream**
> **6 scoops chocolate ice cream**
> **6 scoops choc-chip ice cream**

brownie base

> **250 g/8 oz butter, melted**
> **4 eggs, lightly beaten**
> **1 1/2 cups/330 g/ 10 1/2 oz caster sugar**
> **2 teaspoons vanilla essence**
> **3/4 cup/90 g/3 oz flour, sifted**
> **1/4 cup/30 g/1 oz cocoa powder, sifted**
> **60 g/20 oz chopped dates**
> **45 g/1 1/2 oz chopped pecans**

fudge sauce

> **2 cups/350 g/11 oz brown sugar**
> **1/4 cup/30 g/1 oz cocoa powder, sifted**
> **1 cup/250 ml/8 fl oz thickened double cream**
> **2 tablespoons butter**

tip from the chef

Extra fudge sauce can be stored in an airtight container in the refrigerator.

filled
chocolate cups

■ ■ ■ | Cooking time: 0 minutes - Preparation time: 60 minutes

ingredients
> 440 g/14 oz milk
chocolate, melted

peach cream
> 1¼ cups/315 ml/
10 fl oz cream (double)
> 2 tablespoons icing sugar,
sifted
> 2 peaches, peeled, stoned
and flesh puréed
> ¼ cup/60 ml/2 fl oz
passion fruit pulp

peach coulis
> 3 peaches, peeled, stoned
and flesh puréed
> ⅓ cup/90 ml/3 fl oz
passion fruit pulp
> sugar

method
1. To make chocolate cups, cut six 15 cm/6 in squares of nonstick baking paper. Place small moulds or ramekins upside down on a tray and cover with paper squares. Spoon chocolate over base of mould and allow to run down sides of paper. Spread chocolate with a small spatula if it does not run freely. Allow chocolate to set, then carefully peel off paper.
2. To make peach cream, place cream in a bowl and beat until soft peaks form. Fold in icing sugar, peach purée and passion fruit pulp.
3. To make coulis, push peach purée and passion fruit pulp through a sieve to make a smooth purée. Add sugar to taste. To assemble, flood serving plates with coulis, place chocolate cups on plates and fill with peach cream.

....
Serves 6

tip from the chef
This dessert is delicious garnished with crushed praline. To make praline, place 1 cup/250 g/8 oz sugar and 1 cup/250 ml/8 fl oz water in a saucepan and cook over a low heat, stirring, until sugar dissolves. Increase heat and simmer until syrup is golden. Scatter 3 tablespoons slivered, toasted almonds on a greased baking tray, then pour over toffee. Allow to harden then break into pieces. Place in a food processor and process until toffee resembles coarse breadcrumbs.

chocolate
self-saucing pudding

■■□ | Cooking time: 40 minutes - Preparation time: 30 minutes

method

1. Sift together flour, baking powder and cocoa powder in a bowl. Add caster sugar and mix to combine. Make a well in the centre of the dry ingredients, add milk and butter and mix well to combine. Pour mixture into greased 4 cup/1 litre/1³/4 pt-capacity ovenproof dish.

2. To make sauce, place brown sugar and cocoa powder in a bowl. Gradually add water and mix until smooth. Carefully pour sauce over mixture in dish.

3. Bake at 180°C/350°F/Gas 4 for 40 minutes or until cake is cooked when tested with skewer. Serve scoops of pudding with some of the sauce from the base of the dish and top with a scoop of vanilla or chocolate ice cream.

ingredients

> 1 cup/125 g/4 oz all purpose flour
> ³/4 teaspoon baking powder
> ¹/4 cup/30 g/1 oz cocoa powder
> ³/4 cup/170 g/5¹/2 oz caster sugar
> ¹/2 cup/125 ml/4 fl oz milk
> 45 g/1¹/2 oz butter, melted

chocolate sauce

> ³/4 cup/125 g/4 oz brown sugar
> ¹/4 cup/30 g/1 oz cocoa powder, sifted
> 1¹/4 cups/315 ml/ 10 fl oz hot water

....
Serves 6

tip from the chef

To make the dessert irresistibly crunchier, top with crushed hazelnuts slightly roasted in a clean frying pan.

tuile cups with white chocolate

■ ■ ■ | Cooking time: 5 minutes - Preparation time: 70 minutes

ingredients

- > 125 g/4 oz butter, melted
- > 4 egg whites
- > 2 tablespoons milk
- > 1 cup/125 g/4 oz flour
- > 2/3 cup/140 g/4¹/2 oz caster sugar
- > 60 g/2 oz flaked almonds

white chocolate filling

- > 250 g/8 oz white chocolate, broken into pieces
- > 60 g/2 oz butter, chopped
- > ¹/4 cup/60 ml/2 fl oz cream (double)

tip from the chef

To avoid tuiles from softening, add the filling just before serving. The empty tuiles can be stored in sealed jars up to 2 months.

method

1. To make tuiles, place butter, egg whites, milk, flour and sugar in a bowl (a) and beat until smooth.
2. Place 2 teaspoons of mixture (b) on a lightly greased baking tray and spread out to make a 10 cm/4 in round. Repeat with remaining mixture leaving 10 cm/4 in between each tuile. Sprinkle with almonds and bake at 160°C/325°F/Gas 3 for 3-5 minutes or until edges of tuiles are golden. Using a spatula, carefully remove tuiles from trays and place over a small upturned strainer. Press gently to shape, then allow to cool (c) and harden before removing from strainer.
3. To make filling, place chocolate, butter and cream in a heatproof bowl set over a saucepan of simmering water and heat, stirring, until mixture is smooth. Remove bowl from pan and set aside until mixture thickens slightly. Beat mixture until light and thick. Spoon mixture into a piping bag and pipe into tuile cups.

....
Makes 28

a

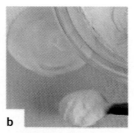

b

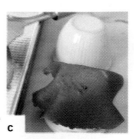

c

chocolate
soufflé

a

b

■ ■ ■ I Cooking time: 35 minutes - Preparation time: 60 minutes

method

1. Place chocolate and half the cream in a heatproof bowl (a) set over a saucepan of simmering water and heat, stirring constantly, until mixture is smooth. Remove bowl from pan and set aside to cool slightly.

2. Place egg yolks and caster sugar in a clean bowl and beat until thick and pale. Gradually beat in flour and remaining cream and beat until combined (b).

3. Transfer egg-yolk mixture to a saucepan and cook over a medium heat, stirring constantly, for 5 minutes or until mixture thickens. Remove pan from heat and stir in chocolate mixture (c,d).

4. Place egg whites in a clean bowl and beat until stiff peaks form. Fold egg whites into chocolate mixture (e). Divide mixture evenly between six buttered and sugared 1 cup/250 ml/8 fl oz-capacity soufflé dishes and bake at 190°C/375°F/Gas 5 for 25 minutes or until soufflés are puffed. Dust with icing sugar, if desired, and serve immediately.

ingredients

> **250 g/8 oz dark chocolate, broken into pieces**
> **1 cup/250 ml/8 fl oz thickened double cream**
> **6 eggs, separated**
> **1 cup/220 g/7 oz caster sugar**
> **¹/₄ cup/30 g/1 oz flour**
> **icing sugar, sifted (optional)**

tip from the chef

To prepare soufflé dishes, brush interior of each with melted unsalted butter, coating lightly and evenly, then sprinkle lightly with caster sugar to coat.

Serves 6

c

d

e

chocolate
ice cream

■■□ | Cooking time: 5 minutes - Preparation time: 40 minutes

ingredients
> 1 cup/220g/7oz caster sugar
> 9 egg yolks
> 1/2 cup/45 g/1 1/2 oz cocoa powder, sifted
> 2 cups/500 ml/16 fl oz milk
> 2 1/2 cups/600 ml/1 pt thickened cream
> 125 g/4 oz milk chocolate, melted

method
1. Place sugar and egg yolks in a bowl and beat until thick and pale (a).
2. Place cocoa powder in a saucepan. Gradually stir in milk and cream and heat over a medium heat, stirring constantly, until mixture is almost boiling. Stir in chocolate (b).
3. Remove pan from heat and whisk hot milk mixture into egg mixture (c). Set aside to cool.
4. Pour mixture into a freezerproof container and freeze for 30 minutes, or until mixture begins to freeze around edges. Beat mixture until even in texture. Return to freezer and repeat beating process two more times. Freeze until solid. Alternatively, place mixture in an ice cream maker and freeze according to manufacturer's instructions.

Makes approximately 7 cups/1750 ml/3 pt

tip from the chef
For true chocoholics, chopped chocolate or chocolate bits can be folded into the mixture before it freezes solid. Serve in scoops with vanilla tuiles or raspberries.

a

b

c

chocolate
brandy ice cream

■□□ | Cooking time: 5 minutes - Preparation time: 40 minutes

method

1. Combine the cream, milk, chocolate and coffee in a large saucepan over moderate heat. Stir until the chocolate melts, do not allow mixture to boil.

2. Meanwhile, using an electric mixer, beat egg yolks with sugar until pale and thick. Continue to beat while adding hot mocha cream. Return mixture to a clean pan and stir constantly over moderate heat until mixture thickens slightly. Stir in brandy. Set aside until cool.

3. Pour mixture into an ice cream maker and chill according to instructions. Alternatively, freeze in ice trays. When semi-frozen, beat mixture to break up any large ice crystals. Repeat the process twice more, then freeze in a suitable container until solid.

Serves 12

ingredients

> **750 ml/ 1¼ pt double cream**
> **250 ml/8 fl oz milk**
> **155 g/5 oz dark chocolate, grated**
> **2 teaspoons instant coffee powder**
> **5 egg yolks**
> **185 g/6 oz caster sugar**
> **2 tablespoons brandy**

tip from the chef

As an altenative to home-made ice cream, you can serve a quick chocolate chip ice cream. Whip 250 ml/8 fl oz double cream with 3 tablespoons Kalhua until soft peaks form; fold mixture into 2 liters/3¹/₂ pt good quality vanilla ice cream, softened. Spoon into a freezerproof container and freeze until semi-frozen. Beat mixture to break up any large ice crystals. Stir in 250 g/8 oz chocolate chips and 125 g/4 oz almonds, chopped. Freeze until solid.

frozen
nutty choc terrine

■■■ I Cooking time: 10 minutes - Preparation time: 60 minutes

method

1. In a large heatproof bowl, melt milk chocolate with the chocolate and hazelnut spread. Cool slightly, stir in Tia Maria and egg yolks. Whip half the cream until soft peaks form. Fold into chocolate mixture.

2. Beat egg whites in a bowl until soft peaks form. Gradually add sugar, beating until mixture is stiff.

3. Melt dark chocolate; fold half into creamy chocolate mixture, then fold in the egg whites. Keep remaining chocolate warm over hot water.

4. Spoon mixture into a large loaf tin lined with cling film. Freeze until firm.

5. Make sauce by adding the remaining cream to the reserved chocolate. Stir over low heat until smooth. Serve with the sliced terrine.

ingredients

> **300 g/9^{1}/$_2$ oz milk chocolate**
> **250 g/8 oz chocolate and hazelnut spread**
> **60 ml/2 fl oz Tia Maria**
> **6 eggs, separated**
> **600 ml/1 pt double cream**
> **3 tablespoons caster sugar**
> **250 g/8 oz dark chocolate**

Serves 12

tip from the chef

To turn this simple terrine into a frozen cake, cover the pan with a baked Swiss roll dough before filling it with the chocolate sauce.

chocolate
pear bombe

■■□ | Cooking time: 5 minutes - Preparation time: 90 minutes

ingredients

> 500 ml/1 pt chocolate ice cream
> 1 1/2 litre/1 1/2 quarts vanilla ice cream
> whipped light cream and chocolate shavings for garnish (optional)

pear ice milk

> 1/3 cup/85 ml/3 oz sugar
> 2 tablespoons lemon juice
> 1 tablespoon pear-flavored liqueur
> 1 tablespoon grated lemon zest
> 850 ml/29 oz canned pear halves, packed in natural juice or water, drained, puréed and chilled

method

1. To make pear ice milk, in a saucepan heat sugar with 1/3 cup/85 ml water until sugar melts. Remove from heat and cool. Add lemon juice, liqueur, and lemon zest. Chill. Stir sugar syrup into chilled pear purée. Transfer to an ice cream machine and freeze according to manufacturer's instructions. Let ice milk "ripen" in freezer for several hours.

2. Chill a 1 1/2 liter/1 1/2 quart mold in the freezer for several hours or overnight. Press three quarters of the chocolate ice cream into the mold, evenly covering the sides and bottom. Cover with plastic film, pressing against the ice cream to seal it tightly and fill any air pockets. Freeze until firm.

3. Press the vanilla ice cream into an even layer over the chocolate ice cream. Cover and freeze until very firm.

4. Fill in the center of the bombe with the pear ice milk. Freeze until very firm.

5. Cover the top surface with the remaining chocolate ice cream. Cover with plastic film and freeze overnight or until ice cream is very firm.

6. To unmould, dip mold quickly in lukewarm water and invert onto a chilled serving plate. Return to freezer to set. Before serving, decorate the bombe with whipped cream and chocolate shavings, if used.

tip from the chef

This elegant bombe boasts two luscious ice-milk layers surrounding a creamy pear sorbet center.

Serves 10

a

b

chocolate
rolls

■■□ | Cooking time: 20 minutes - Preparation time: 25 minutes

method

1. Place egg yolks and sugar in a mixing bowl and beat until mixture is thick and creamy. Beat in chocolate, then fold in flour mixture.
2. Beat egg whites until stiff peaks form (a) and fold into chocolate mixture. Pour into a greased and lined 26 x 32 cm/10½ x 12¾ in Swiss roll tin and bake at 180°C/350°F/Gas 4 for 12-15 minutes or until just firm. Turn onto a damp teatowel sprinkled with caster sugar and roll up from the short end (b). Set aside to cool.
3. To make filling, place chocolate and cream in a small saucepan and cook over a low heat until chocolate melts and mixture is well blended. Bring to the boil, remove from heat and set aside to cool completely. When cold, place in a mixing bowl over ice and beat until thick and creamy.
4. Unroll cake, spread with filling and reroll (c). To serve, cut into slices.

ingredients

> 5 eggs, separated
> ¼ cup/60 g/2 oz caster sugar
> 100 g/3½ oz dark chocolate, melted and cooled
> 2 tablespoons self-raising flour, sifted with 2 tablespoons cocoa powder

chocolate filling

> 60 g/2 oz dark chocolate
> 2/3 cup/170 ml/ 5½ fl oz cream (double)

Serves 8

tip from the chef

A chocolate roll filled with chocolate cream makes a special afternoon tea treat or dessert. Irresistibly good to eat, these spectacular cakes are easy to make. Follow these step-by-step instructions for a perfect result every time.

c

fruit
and nut brownies

■ ■ ■ | Cooking time: 50 minutes - Preparation time: 60 minutes

ingredients
> **125 g/4 oz dark chocolate, chopped**
> **90 g/3 oz butter**
> **2 eggs**
> **1¹/4 cups/280 g/9 oz caster sugar**
> **60 g/2 oz walnuts, chopped**
> **90 g/3 oz chocolate-coated sultanas or raisins**
> **¹/2 cup/60 g/2 oz self-raising flour, sifted**

chocolate topping
> **90 g/3 oz dark chocolate, chopped**
> **185 g/6 oz cream cheese**
> **2 tablespoons sugar**
> **1 egg**

method
1. Place chocolate and butter in a heatproof bowl set over a saucepan of simmering water and cook, stirring constantly, until chocolate and butter melt and mixture is combined. Remove bowl from heat and set aside to cool slightly.
2. Place eggs and caster sugar in a bowl and beat until foamy. Fold chocolate mixture, walnuts, sultanas or raisins and flour into egg mixture. Spoon batter into a greased and lined 23 cm/9 in springform tin and bake at 160°C/325°F/Gas 3 for 40 minutes or until top is dry but center is still moist.
3. To make topping, place chocolate in a heatproof bowl set over a saucepan of simmering water and heat until chocolate melts. Remove bowl from heat and set aside to cool slightly. Place cream cheese and sugar in a bowl and beat until smooth. Beat in egg, then chocolate mixture and continue beating until well combined. Pour topping over hot brownies and bake for 15 minutes longer. Allow to cool in tin, then refrigerate for 2 hours before cutting into wedges and serving.

....
Serves 10

tip from the chef
Two of the easiest decorations for a baked product are chocolate curls and shavings. Curls are made from chocolate at room temperature; for shavings the chocolate is chilled first. Using a vegetable peeler, shave the sides of the block of chocolate. Curls or shavings will form depending on the temperature of the chocolate.

marbled
shells

■ ■ ■ | Cooking time: 6 minutes - Preparation time: 90 minutes

ingredients

> 200 g/6¹/2 oz dark chocolate, melted
> 200 g/6¹/2 oz white chocolate, melted

creamy chocolate filling

> 200 g/6¹/2 oz milk chocolate
> ¹/2 cup/125 ml/4 fl oz thickened double cream
> 2 tablespoons coffee-flavored or hazelnut-flavored liqueur

tip from the chef

Do not overmix the white and dark chocolates or the marbled effect will diminish. Make sure the first coating sets completely before adding the filling so that the first coating does not crack.

method

1. To make filling, place milk chocolate, cream and liqueur in a heatproof bowl set over a saucepan of simmering water and heat, stirring, until mixture is smooth. Remove bowl from pan and set aside until mixture cools and thickens.

2. Place a teaspoon of dark chocolate and a teaspoon of white chocolate in a shell-shaped chocolate mold. Swirl with a skewer (a) to marble chocolate and using a small brush, brush chocolate evenly over mold. Tap mold gently on work surface to remove any air bubbles. Repeat with remaining chocolate to make 30 molds. Freeze for 2 minutes or until chocolate sets.

3. Place a small spoonful of filling (b) in each chocolate shell. Spoon equal quantities of the remaining dark and white chocolate over filling (c) to fill mold. Using a skewer, carefully swirl chocolate to give marbled effect. Tap mold gently on work surface. Freeze for 3 minutes or until chocolate sets. Tap molds gently to remove chocolates.

....
Makes 30

a

b

c

truffle
easter eggs

■ ■ ■ | Cooking time: 5 minutes - Preparation time: 90 minutes

method

1. Place a spoonful of dark chocolate in a small Easter egg mold and use a small paintbrush to evenly coat. Freeze for 2 minutes or until chocolate sets. Repeat with remaining chocolate to make 32 shells.

2. To make filling, place cream in a saucepan and bring to the boil. Remove pan from heat, add milk chocolate and stir until smooth. Stir in golden syrup and chill for 20 minutes or until mixture is thick enough to pipe.

3. Spoon filling into a piping bag fitted with a star-shaped nozzle and pipe filling into chocolate shells.

ingredients

> **125 g/4 oz dark chocolate, melted**

truffle filling

> **¹/2 cup/125 ml/4 fl oz thickened double cream**
> **250 g/8 oz milk chocolate**
> **1 tablespoon golden syrup**

Makes 32

tip from the chef

Eggs can be moulded and filled several hours in advance. Store in a covered container in a cool, dry place.

ice cream
christmas pudding

■□□ I Cooking time: 0 minutes - Preparation time: 30 minutes

method

1. Place ice cream, apricots, cherries, pears, sultanas, raisins and rum in a bowl and mix to combine. Pour into an oiled and lined 6 cup/1.5 liter/2¹/₂ pt-capacity pudding basin.
2. Freeze for 3 hours or until firm. To serve, slice pudding and serve with rum custard.

Serves 8

ingredients

- > **1 liter/ 1³/4 pt chocolate ice cream, softened**
- > **125 g/4 oz glacé apricots, chopped**
- > **125 g/4 oz glacé cherries, chopped**
- > **125 g/4 oz glacé pears, chopped**
- > **90 g/3 oz sultanas**
- > **75 g/2¹/2 oz raisins, chopped**
- > **2 tablespoons rum**

tip from the chef

To help unmould the pudding, briefly hold a warm damp teatowel around the outside of the mold.

index